I'd Kill To Be a Widow
Reflections on Divorce

Illustrations by Ann W. Kavanagh

ISBN 1-56875-064-1

For inquiries, correspondence or information regarding
bulk purchases,
please contact:

Betty Catron
P.O. Box 11174
Knoxville, TN 37939

Third printing, March 1995

DEDICATION

This little book is dedicated to all first wives who did it all and are now alone. The women who married young and forever. They loved, they raised the children. They were the helpmate through the lean years, saved for the golden years. They turned the other cheek, forgave and overlooked. The ones who really tried to stick it out, in the very best sense of the word.

Peace to us all.

Hire a tenacious, smart, moral, male attorney — who returns calls.
This will be your lifeline

A wise aunt put it all in perspective — you don't want to be with someone who doesn't want to be with you. It's really that simple.

When one door closes,
another opens — but
you may have to knock

Life is not fair,
never was,

never will be

Lean on Friends

Keep a sense of humor

Plot murder,
but think twice
before taking
action

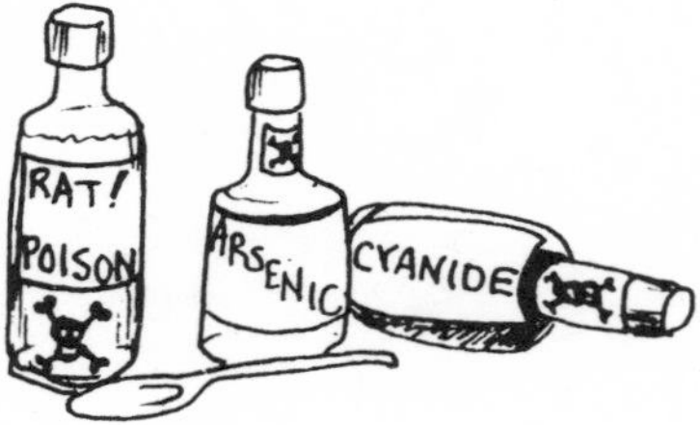

Leave the children out.
It's impossible, but
give it a try.

Stay in your home,
if you love it.
Move if you don't

Don't look for fair
treatment from male
judges or female attorneys

What goes around
comes around,
I hope

Don't listen to easy-
listening radio stations

Keep Busy

Money is not everything,
but it's close

Forgiveness is between yourself and God. Don't tell the world, much less the forgiven

Love without trust
is like driving without
wearing a seat belt.

Don't make any major decisions for two years after the divorce is final.

Set goals:

Daily, weekly. yearly.

lifely

Divide and Distribute
to the children
all family pictures

Be prepared to go to trial,
many settlements are made
on the courthouse steps.

Don't trust private detectives
that drive long, black
cars and wear lots
of gold.

The best private
detectives are called
C. P. A.'s

Know that being alone
is not the same
as being lonely

Look
for
a
Silver
Lining

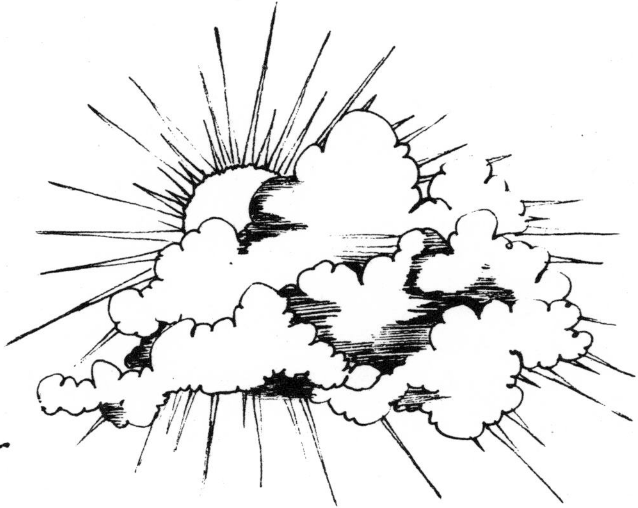

I had an acquaintance ask
"How's your family?"

"My family's great," I
answered, "It's just
one smaller."

Be kind to yourself.

Don't go
to
Singles bars

C. O. B. R. A.
is not
just a snake
in India

Single women dont
have P. M. S.

Know early on there will be
times you will want to lie
down and never wake up.
Not really suicide — just
the tiredness that comes
from pain

The greatest gift a father can give his children is to love their mother.

Go with gut feelings

Don't join a 12-step program

It's always darkest before the dawn — also you can watch Cher give beauty advice.

If you cant sleep -
try Excedrin P.M.

Don't buy into co-dependency or enabling – they are just excuses to make unacceptable behavior acceptable.

Holidays are hard. Don't feel sorry for yourself. Donate your time where it is accepted without question — nursing homes, shelters, children's hospitals.

If you're under psychiatric
care and have to apply
for health insurance.
you are flat out of luck

An adulterer with a
clear conscience is
capable of anything.

Be leery of psychiatrists
and psychologists.
Many are crazy.

Don't give back any jewelry
— have it redesigned

Fool me once - shame on you
Fool me twice - shame on me

Three people cant make
a marriage — but they
can a divorce.

you'll gain closet space

Beware of "sweetness" in mothers-in-law. It masks resentment.

My personal feeling on forgiveness is that it only encourages those doing the sinning.

Have a male friend
to talk with. It will
restore your faith that
all men are not egotistical,
selfish jerks.

Keep all evidence, no
matter how insignificant
it seems at the time.
Keep all letters. Keep a
log of all strange phone
calls.

Words are cheap. Look
only to actions. Rarely
do people change.

Remember, in this process indifference is the opposite of love

When enough is enough,
you'll know it !!!

Keep on Keeping On

Exercise

Widows are so lucky.

There's no such thing as
a friendly divorce

Hang-up calls are from the other woman

Tell your friends — enough already with the ex-husband-sighting reports.

The way to a man's heart
is not through his
stomach.

Have old-fashioned
slumber parties

Have friends to dinner

Get a security system
and use it

Rely on yourself. Know that if you were not strong, self-sufficient and self-respecting, you wouldn't be here.

Dependent women don't get divorced.

Become a Grandmother

Be patient—time is your
ally.

If the other woman is
ugly as sin, you know
what her strong
suit is.

Doctors are not Gods, no matter what the medical books say

Mental abuse is evil

I never really knew
what a Ms. was —
now I are one

Find pleasure in simple things

If you're afraid of the dark, best stay married

Children's weddings will be
the pits. Handle them with
grace — they will be your
finest hour

It's OK to go to movies alone !

Have a reason to begin
each day. Get a job or
volunteer. Best get up
and get out and get going

When I told my 75 year old mother all that had happened, that I was filing for divorce and was really ready to kill him, she said "Don't even talk that way. You're still young with a good life ahead of you. .... I'll do it!"

Manipulative men are
often whiny, poor-
pitiful-wimps

Broken hearts heal but
there will be scar tissue

Don't count on re-marrying
The men our age are out
dating our daughters

Terminal illness isn't
what it used to be

Do everything your conscience will allow to save your marriage and if that fails you will never look back and ask, "What if?"

Change your vocabulary
from we and ours
to me and mine

If your husband has a Swiss bank account, best be suspicious

You'll find out who
your real friends are

Husbands think they are only leaving their wives, but they are also leaving their children, their friends, their in-laws, their neighbors, their un-born grandchildren - who will someday look at a picture and ask, "Who's that?"

Keep cooking

Divorce is like being fired from a job you hate

Take care of your car

My fantasy singles—
Column ad:

DWF with new power-
washer desires meeting
eligible male with
comparable tool.

The reply: Send picture of
power-washer

Somehow I thought being a Girl Scout Cookie chairman would reap greater rewards

CHOCOLATE MINT
G S
COOKIES

BUTTER CREAM
G S
COOKIES

The "F" word will roll
from your lips with ease.
and somehow it's just so
appropriate. Don't worry —
you'll clean up your
act later.

If you never flirted
with your friend's husband
— don't start now

Be totally honest with
your Lawyer

Life would be far simpler
if triangulation only
referred to surveys

Second chances are wonderful
to give, but once given,
taken lightly and
squandered away—the
giver becomes a fool and
the taker a thief

I don't even have a friend
I want to die so I can
marry her husband

If you really need
to be welcomed home,
get a dog

Life goes on — so go on
with it. Don't get
left behind

Look good
and
Keep Smiling

Faithful husbands

Don't lose wedding rings

Paint up, fix up, clean up
the things around you.
Their renewal will parallel
your own.

You can count on sympathy for just so long. Even good friends will tire of the sordid details. After awhile just shut up.

The family that plays
together stays together.
Sounds great - but it is
a myth.

If it perks your spirit,
dye your hair - but
avoid orange and purple

The process of divorce
is all - consuming

Adultery may be a symptom
of a problem marriage — but
anyone with half a brain
should know if you don't treat
the symptom first, the cure
may not be worth the pain

Go to Church

Get rid of all physical
reminders of your ex.
Many Gitman Brothers
shirts on the backs of
homeless men in my hometown

Build fires just for yourself

Patience. Patience. Patience
This too shall pass.

Don't assume the role of mind-reader

When your husband cancels your health insurance, Car insurance, and doesn't pay the mortgage, count yourself lucky if Southern Living still gets through

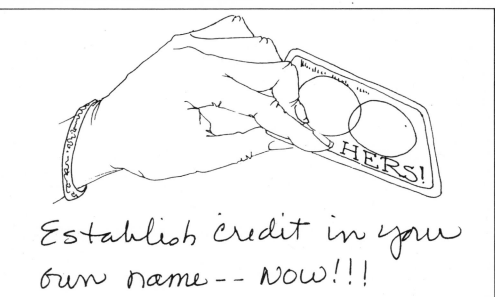

Establish credit in your
own name -- NOW!!!

Keep your house in Order

When you burn the last
bridge, use gasoline
and a blowtorch

Buy new underwear

Remember always, for every philandering husband there's at least one accommodating woman

Bait Your
Own
Hook

ABOUT THE AUTHOR

I'm still in my home; I became a grandmother; I play some golf; I read a lot; I walk everyday with my buddies; I have friends to dinner; I work full-time in real estate in Knoxville; I've lost touch with some friends, but I've gained so many more. Life is different from what I thought it would be for so many years, but it's peaceful and for that I'm thankful.

Betty Catron

ABOUT THE ILLUSTRATOR

I experienced the subject of this book in the early '70's and after considerable adjustment time, remet a childhood sweetheart. We were married in 1979. There is a rainbow after all!! My husband is kind, generous, handsome, smart and funny, etc. We live in south Alabama on Mobile Bay where we sail, fly, travel and laugh. We share 5 great children, two with spouses, and their adventures. I teach art at a local high school, and in my limited spare time, enjoy painting, cooking and photography.

Ann W. Kavanagh